Jerry West

THE STORY OF THE LOS ANGELES LAKERS

Michael Cooper

A HISTORY OF HOOPS

THE STORY OF THE

LOS ANGELES LAKERS

JIM WHITING

Magic Johnson

CREATIVE EDUCATION / CREATIVE PAPERBACKS

CREATIVE SPORTS

Published by Creative Education and Creative Paperbacks
P.O. Box 227, Mankato, Minnesota 56002
Creative Education and Creative Paperbacks are imprints of
The Creative Company
www.thecreativecompany.us

Design and production by Blue Design (www.bluedes.com)
Art direction by Rita Marshall
Production layout by Rachel Klimpel and Ciara Beitlich

Photographs by AP Images (Michael Tweed), Getty (Robyn Beck, Andrew D
Bernstein, Bettmann, Lisa Blumenfeld, Steph Chambers, Kevork Djansezian,
Noah Graham, Otto Greule Jr., Robert Laberge, George Long, Richard
Mackson, MediaNews Group/Pasadena Star-News, Peter Read Miller, NBA
Photos, Mike Powell, Ezra Shaw, Wally Skalij), Newscom (Icon Sports Media,
John W. McDonough/Icon SMI, Jim Ruymen), Shutterstock (Brocreative,
Andrey Burmakin, Valentin Valkov), US Presswire (Manny Rubio), Wikimedia
Commons (Bettmann, The Sporting News Archives)

Library of Congress Cataloging-in-Publication Data
Names: Whiting, Jim, 1943- author.
Title: The story of the Los Angeles Lakers / by Jim Whiting.
Description: Mankato, Minnesota : Creative Education/Creative
    Paperbacks, 2023. | Series: Creative Sports. A History of Hoops | Includes
    index. | Audience: Ages 8-12 | Audience: Grades 4-6 | Summary: "Middle
    grade basketball fans are introduced to the extraordinary history of
    NBA's L.A. Lakers with a photo-laden narrative of their greatest successes
    and losses"-- Provided by publisher.
Identifiers: LCCN 2022009496 (print) | LCCN 2022009497 (ebook) | ISBN
    9781640266308 (library binding) | ISBN 9781682771860 (paperback) | ISBN
    9781640007710 (ebook)
Subjects: LCSH: Los Angeles Lakers (Basketball team)--History--Juvenile
    literature.
Classification: LCC GV885.52.L67 W453 2023 (print) | LCC GV885.52.L67
    (ebook) | DDC 796.323/640979494--dc23/eng/20220224
LC record available at https://lccn.loc.gov/2022009496
LC ebook record available at https://lccn.loc.gov/2022009497

Elgin Baylor

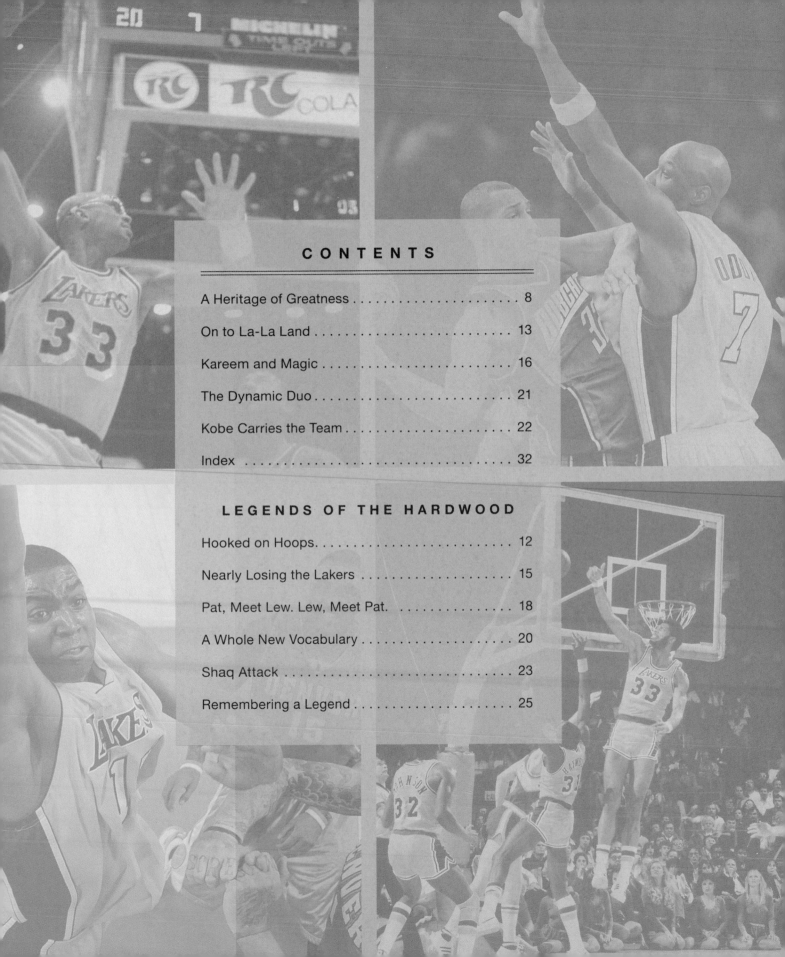

CONTENTS

LEGENDS OF THE HARDWOOD

A HERITAGE OF GREATNESS

On January 22, 2006, few people were tuned into the National Basketball Association (NBA) game between the Toronto Raptors and the Los Angeles Lakers. The conference championship games of the National Football League were also playing, and the winners would go to the Super Bowl. However, that NBA game became famous for Kobe Bryant's high-scoring record. "They [the Lakers] had Kobe and a bunch of guys," play-by-play commentator Bill Macdonald said. "We knew for them to be in any game, Kobe was going to have to go completely nuts."

Toronto took a 14-point lead at halftime. Lakers star shooting guard Bryant had 26 points at that point. That was fine with the Raptors. "He's killing us, but the rest of the team is doing nothing, and we're winning. We didn't think he would keep scoring like he was," said Toronto guard Jose Calderon.

Calderon was wrong. Two minutes into the third quarter, Toronto extended its lead to 69–51. At that point Bryant started "to go completely nuts." He scored 13 points in the next 3 minutes. A slam dunk near the end of the quarter put the Lakers ahead by two points. In all, Bryant had 27 points in that quarter. In the fourth quarter, he scored a whopping 20 points in the game's final 6 minutes. Bryant had recorded 55 points in the second half. That was 14 more than the entire Toronto team. He finished with 81 points. Only Wilt Chamberlain, with 100 in 1962, has had more points in a single game. The Lakers won, 122–104.

Kobe Bryant

One reporter asked Bryant if he had ever imagined a game like this. "Never," he said. "Not even in my dreams. It's just something that kind of just, happened." Yet he wasn't satisfied. Years later, he watched a video of the game for the first time. "Watching the game now, the easy shots I missed, I could of had 100 [points]!" he wrote on Twitter.

Bryant is the latest in a long line of Lakers superstars that stretches back to the team's founding in 1947. The Detroit Gems of the National Basketball League (NBL) had just folded. Two Minneapolis businessmen bought the team. Many people call Minnesota the "Land of 10,000 Lakes," so the owners called the team the Lakers. The Gems had ended with the league's worst record. The Lakers demanded the first choice in a special draft of players from another failed team. They chose 6-foot-10 center George Mikan. He became the league's first dominant big man, towering over small players. The Lakers won the NBL championship. The following year, the team joined the rival Basketball Association of America (BAA). They won that league championship, too. Mikan's scoring and defense were the keys.

The NBL and BAA merged before the 1949–50 season to form the NBA. Minneapolis won the championship that season as well. In 1950–51, they faced the Rochester Royals in the division finals. Mikan played with a fractured leg. He said, "I couldn't run, sort of hopped down the court." The Lakers lost to the Royals that season but surged back to win the NBA title the next three years.

Mikan was key to the Lakers' success. Once, a sign outside the arena in New York City read "Geo. Mikan vs. Knicks" before a game. When Mikan walked into the locker room, his teammates were still in street clothes. "They're advertising you're playing against the Knicks, so go play them," one of them joked. "We'll wait here."

Vern Mikkelsen

LEGENDS
OF THE HARDWOOD

Minneapolis Lakers – 1950

GEORGE MIKAN
CENTER
HEIGHT: 6-FOOT
LAKERS SEASONS
1947–54, 1956

HOOKED ON HOOPS

Growing up, George Mikan was an unlikely
candidate for stardom. He wore thick eyeglasses.
He shattered a knee when he was young and
spent a year and a half in bed. In high school, he
wanted to be a priest. He stood 6-foot-10 but had
never played basketball. In that era, players his
size were considered too clumsy. All that changed
when he went to DePaul University. Coach Ray
Meyer took him under his wing. "Mikan was really
bad to start with," said the first-year coach.
"He was so awkward." Meyer saw his potential.
He taught Mikan how to shoot a hook shot with
either hand. It made him almost unstoppable.
Mikan was a three-time All-American in college
and was voted the top player of the first half of
the 20th century. "George dominated the game
like no one did," Meyer said years later."It became
a big man's game."

Mikan's dominance was no joke to the rest of the league. The NBA made several rule changes to reduce his advantages. The foul lane was widened from 6 feet to 12 to limit Mikan's moves under the basket. They also made goaltending illegal to stop Mikan from swatting away shots that might have gone in. There was still another way of slowing him down. Opposing teams kept battering him. All the pounding wore out his body. He retired after the 1954 championship.

ON TO LA-LA LAND

Without Mikan, the Lakers had losing records in three of the next four years. The worst was 1957–58. They won just 19 games. Fans stayed away. The team lost money and was sold to trucking line owner Bob Short. The poor record gave the Lakers the second overall pick in the 1958 NBA Draft. They chose high-flying small forward Elgin Baylor. Fans came back. "It just wasn't the number of points he scored; it was the way he got them, thrilling fans with the remarkable variety of his elegant actions," said ESPN sportswriter Larry Schwartz. He averaged nearly 25 points a game. He was an easy choice for NBA Rookie of the Year.

Baylor powered the team to the 1959 NBA Finals. But the Boston Celtics swept the Lakers. The team won just 25 games the following season, causing a drop in ticket sales again. Short had the idea to move the team to Los Angeles. The Brooklyn Dodgers of Major League Baseball had just moved there, and eager fans poured into their games. Short thought the same thing would happen with the Lakers. He moved the team in 1960. Southern California doesn't have many lakes, but Short decided to keep the team's name.

The team drafted guard Jerry West in 1960. Few people played with more intensity. West broke his nose at least nine times. "He took a loss harder than any player I've ever known," said longtime Lakers broadcaster Chick Hearn. West helped the team to the Western Division finals against the St. Louis Hawks. They took a 3–2 series lead. They lost the next two games by a total of three points.

The Lakers advanced to the NBA Finals again in 1962 against the Celtics. West's last-second shot won Game 3. He always remembered it. "Everyone wants to hit a home run in the ninth inning to win the big game. That was my home run," he said. But the Lakers lost the series, 4 games to 3.

Almost the same thing happened in four of the next six seasons. The Lakers simply couldn't beat the Celtics when it counted most. Boston center Bill Russell controlled the area under the basket. The Lakers didn't have anyone who could keep up. They traded for 7-foot-1 superstar center Wilt Chamberlain in 1968–69. Again, the Lakers and the Celtics met in the Finals. The result was the same. Boston won the decisive Game 7, 108–106. West was named Finals MVP. It is the only time a member of the losing team has won that honor.

In the 1969–70 season, Los Angeles faced the New York Knicks in the Finals. The Lakers lost the series, 4 games to 3. The Lakers continued their regular-season dominance into the 1970–71 season. Guard Gail Goodrich joined West in the backcourt. But they lost to the Milwaukee Bucks in the Western Conference finals.

KAREEM AND MAGIC

Fans were growing impatient. The team had moved from Minneapolis 11 years ago but still hadn't won a championship. Time was running out. Several star players were in their mid-30s. The team hired former Celtics guard Bill Sharman as coach. He ran a fast-break offense and emphasized tough defense. Baylor retired on Halloween, nine games into the 1971–72 season. Five days later, the Lakers began a 33-game winning streak. That is still an NBA record today. They went on to win 69 games that season. It was the most in NBA history at that time. They faced the Knicks for the title. New York knocked off Los Angeles in the first game. The Lakers surged back to win the next four. West finally had his championship ring.

The Knicks turned the tables the following season. They beat the Lakers in the NBA Finals. Los Angeles lost to the Milwaukee Bucks in the first round of the 1973–74 playoffs. West retired. In his 14-year Lakers career, he averaged 27 points a game. Center Kareem Abdul-Jabbar joined Los Angeles the following season. Even though he became the first Laker to be named league MVP, the team missed the playoffs. Something was lacking.

Magic Johnson

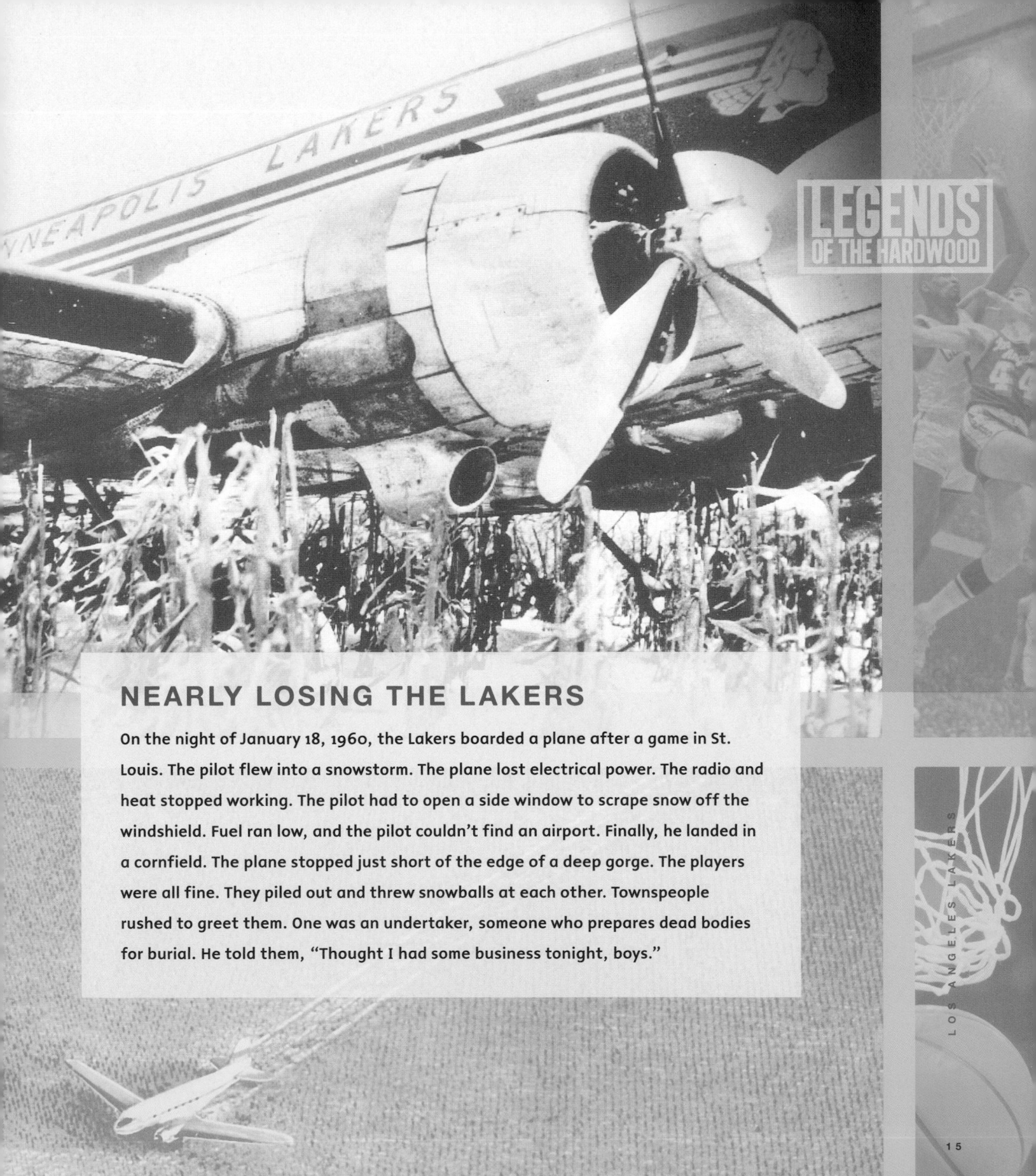

NEARLY LOSING THE LAKERS

On the night of January 18, 1960, the Lakers boarded a plane after a game in St. Louis. The pilot flew into a snowstorm. The plane lost electrical power. The radio and heat stopped working. The pilot had to open a side window to scrape snow off the windshield. Fuel ran low, and the pilot couldn't find an airport. Finally, he landed in a cornfield. The plane stopped just short of the edge of a deep gorge. The players were all fine. They piled out and threw snowballs at each other. Townspeople rushed to greet them. One was an undertaker, someone who prepares dead bodies for burial. He told them, "Thought I had some business tonight, boys."

LOS ANGELES LAKERS

Kareem Abdul-Jabbar

Pat Riley

PAT, MEET LEW. LEW, MEET PAT.

In 1961, Pat Riley's Linton High School (Schenectady, NY) team played Kareem Abdul-Jabbar's Power Memorial squad. Riley was a hot-shooting junior. People called him "The Linton Flash." Abdul-Jabbar (then known as Lew Alcindor before he changed his name) was an awkward, 6-foot-10 freshman. "Jabbar was tall, that's about all you can say for him," said a Linton parent. Riley netted 19 as Linton won 64–58. Alcindor scored just eight. Still, Linton player Bill Boehm said, "You could tell that [Abdul-Jabbar] was going to be the next big player in the game." This game might be the only time that a future Hall of Fame coach and his star player were on the floor at the same time.

That "something" was Earvin "Magic" Johnson, a 6-foot-9 point guard. Basketball had been his life growing up. "I practiced all day," he said. "I dribbled to the store with my right hand and back with my left. Then I slept with my basketball." The Lakers selected Johnson with the top overall pick in the 1979 NBA Draft. The team won 60 games in his first season. Los Angeles took a 3–2 series edge over the Philadelphia 76ers in the NBA Finals. Then Abdul-Jabbar suffered a severe sprained ankle. Los Angeles called on Johnson to replace him even though he had never played center. Johnson scored 42 points, and the Lakers won 123–107 to claim the championship. They defeated the 76ers two years later to take another title.

By now, the Lakers were known as "Showtime" for their exciting style of play. Many highly paid Hollywood stars loved attending games at The Forum, the Lakers' home arena. *The Washington Post* joked, "The Forum may be the only place where the fans make more money than the players." The Lakers gave fans of all income levels their money's worth. They played in the NBA Finals in 1983 and 1984 but lost. They won titles in 1985, 1987, and 1988. Coach Pat Riley was one of the main reasons for this string of success. He was a former Laker who became coach in 1981.

LEGENDS OF THE HARDWOOD

CHICK HEARN
BROADCASTER
1961–2002

A WHOLE NEW VOCABULARY

Chick Hearn was the beloved announcer of Lakers games. He coined many
basketball phrases. He said, "No harm, no foul," when there was minor
contact the referees should ignore. When the refs called a minor contact, he
called it a "ticky-tacky foul." One of the most famous "Chickisms" referred
to a player putting up an impossible shot: "He has two chances, slim and
none, and slim just left the building." People loved Hearn's candor while
broadcasting. During his 3,000th game in 1998, the Lakers weren't playing
well. "The Lakers look like dogs," he told the crowd at halftime. The Lakers
rallied and pulled out a narrow victory. When Hearn died after suffering a
fall in 2002, tributes poured in. "Chick, we'll miss you dearly," said Lakers
general manager Mitch Kupchak. "Quite simply, you're the best."

THE DYNAMIC DUO

The team continued at a high level. They made the NBA Finals two more times but lost. Abdul-Jabbar retired in 1989. Johnson followed two years later. The team had early playoff exits for several years afterward. Los Angeles added two key players for the 1996–97 season. One was massive center Shaquille "Shaq" O'Neal. The team signed him as a free agent. He averaged 26 points a game. The other addition was shooting guard Kobe Bryant. He entered the NBA Draft right after high school. Bryant was named to the NBA All-Rookie First Team even though he wasn't a starter. Despite their contributions, the Lakers made another early playoff exit.

The team won 61 games the following season. The Utah Jazz swept them in the conference finals. The San Antonio Spurs beat them in the conference semifinals the following season.

Things came together in 1999–2000. Phil Jackson became coach. He did some unusual things, such as beating drums on game days. But he knew how to get the best out of his players. The Lakers rushed to the NBA championship, defeating the Indiana Pacers, 4 games to 2. "This is why I came here," O'Neal said. "I wanted to be a champion." He swept the major awards: MVP of the league, Finals MVP, and All-Star Game MVP.

The good times continued. The Lakers lost just one game in a total of four series to win the 2000–01 title. They were almost as dominant the following year. They won their third title in a row by sweeping the New Jersey Nets in the Finals. Fans hoped for a "four-peat." That hadn't happened since the legendary Boston teams of the 1960s. But Los Angeles lost to the Spurs in the conference semifinals in 2003. The next year, they fell to the Detroit Pistons in the Finals, 4 games to 1. Los Angeles traded O'Neal to Miami after the season. Coach Jackson moved on.

KOBE CARRIES THE TEAM

Without those two cornerstones, the Lakers struggled. They won only 34 games in 2004–05. They missed the playoffs for the first time in 11 years. Jackson came back as coach in 2005. The Lakers returned to the playoffs in the next two seasons. Both times they lost in the first round. Los Angeles picked up center/power forward Pau Gasol during the 2007–08 season. The team went 22–5 with him in the lineup. Bryant had his best year ever. He was named league MVP. But the Celtics defeated them for the NBA title. Los Angeles surged to the top in the two following seasons, defeating the Orlando Magic in 2009 and Boston in 2010. Fans hoped for a three-peat in 2011, but the Dallas Mavericks defeated the Lakers in the conference semifinals. Jackson retired for health reasons.

SHAQUILLE O'NEAL
CENTER
HEIGHT: 7-FOOT-1
LAKERS SEASONS:
1996–2004

SHAQ ATTACK

Shaquille O'Neal weighed less than eight pounds when he was born. He quickly began growing. He stood 6-foot-4 when he was 10 years old. His stepfather taught him to use his size to his advantage under the basket rather than backing away from smaller opponents. The lesson helped him become a star in college. In 1992, O'Neal signed the largest rookie contract in NBA history. He helped win four NBA titles, including three with the Lakers. O'Neal hung up his jersey in 2011. His Lakers jersey number 34 is retired. O'Neal has given "active retirement" a whole new meaning. Acting in TV shows and commercials, being a DJ, playing rap music, and pursuing philanthropy are some of the many things that he likes to do.

KOBE BRYANT
SHOOTING GUARD/SMALL FORWARD
HEIGHT: 6-FOOT-6
LAKERS SEASONS: 1996–2016

REMEMBERING A LEGEND

People packed Staples Arena to capacity for Kobe Bryant's final game on April 13, 2016. His teammates focused entirely on getting him the ball. He had a career-high 50 shot attempts and finished with 60 points. He personally outscored the Jazz 23–21 in the last quarter as Los Angeles won, 101–96. Four years later, when Bryant died in a helicopter crash, countless tributes flowed in. Bryant is one of a handful of iconic players—such as Michael Jordan and LeBron James—whose name is instantly recognizable around the world. More than 14,000 babies have been named after him.

LOS ANGELES LAKERS

25

Los Angeles lost to the Oklahoma City Thunder in the conference semifinals the following season. Bryant suffered a torn Achilles tendon near the end of 2012–13. The Spurs swept the Lakers in the first round of the playoffs. Bryant played in only six games the following year due to more injuries. The team managed just 27 wins. He was injured yet again in 2014–15. Los Angeles did even worse, winning only 21 games. Early in the 2015–16 season, Bryant announced he would retire when it was over. The Lakers stumbled to 17 wins. Bryant became the first player to stay with the same team for 20 years.

Los Angeles struggled through two more losing seasons. Then LeBron James stunned the basketball world when he left Cleveland for the second time to sign with the Lakers. "L.A.-Bron," as he was quickly nicknamed, wanted a larger platform for his philanthropy and social activism.

The move wasn't an immediate success. James suffered an early season injury and missed 17 games. The team had signed a number of other newcomers and lacked cohesion. They finished 37–45 and missed the playoffs for the sixth season in a row. For James personally, it ended two streaks: 13 straight years in the playoffs, 8 straight years in the Finals.

Before the 2019–20 season, Los Angeles traded a combination of players and future draft picks to New Orleans for power forward Anthony Davis. The Lakers roared out to a 17–2 start. Even with the season shortened by the COVID-19 pandemic, they still won 52 games and had the top seed in the Western Conference. They won the first three rounds by identical 4–1 series margins. They were nearly as good against the Miami Heat in the Finals, winning 4 games to 2. James became the first player to be named Finals MVP with three different teams.

Anthony Davis

LeBron James

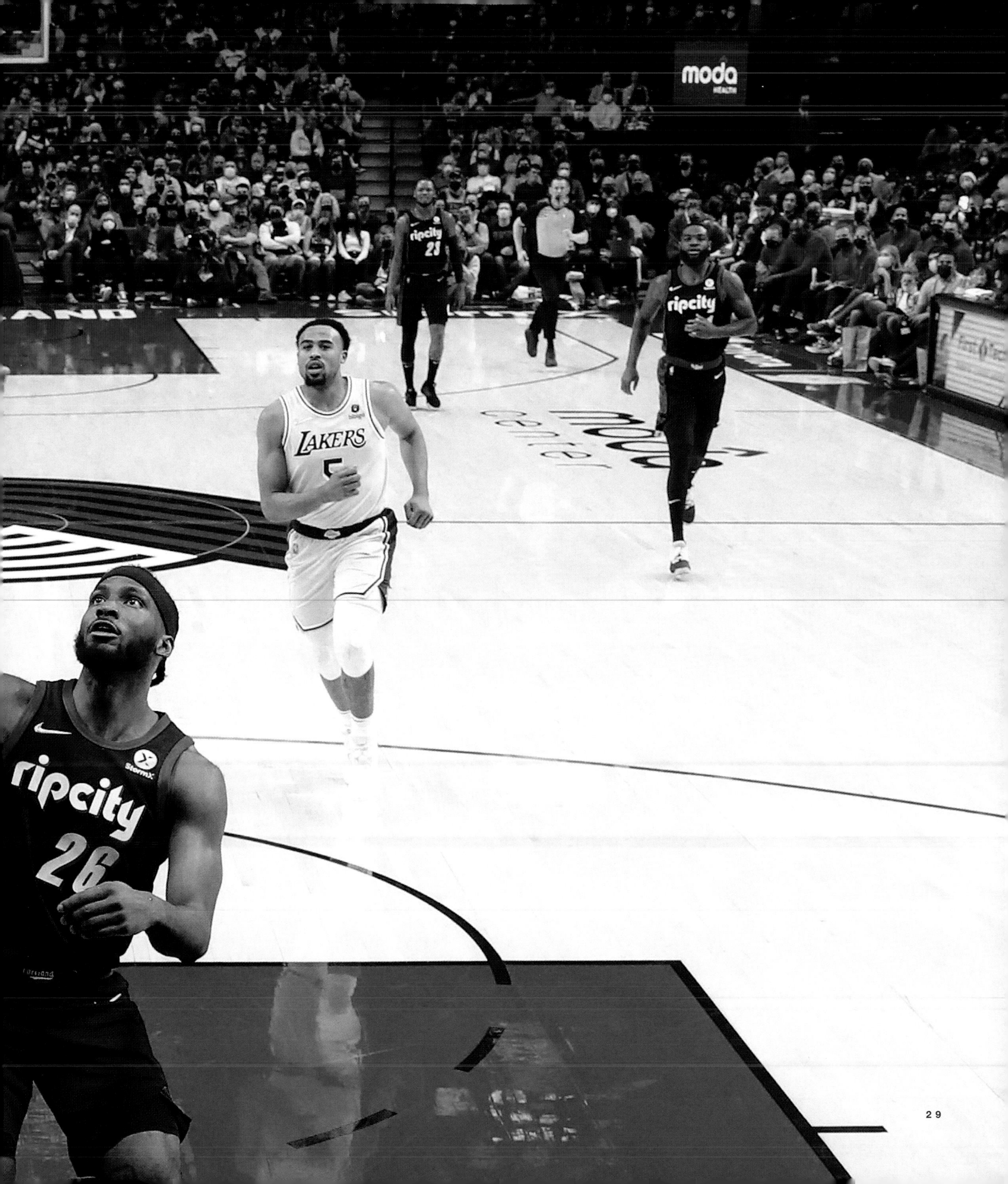
moda
HEALTH
ripcity
23
LAKERS
5
moda
center
ripcity
26

The Lakers suffered a number of injuries but still managed a 42–30 record in 2020–21. They lost in the first round of the playoffs to the Phoenix Suns. The Lakers hoped the injury bug had passed by the 2021–22 season. That wasn't the only concern. The team signed superstar guard Russell Westbrook. They paid him so much there wasn't enough money to contract any role players their defense needed. As Daniel Starkand of LakersNation.com observed, "The biggest part of why the Lakers were so successful the two seasons prior was because they surrounded LeBron James and Anthony Davis with role players who were tough-minded, defense-first players and didn't mind doing all the dirty work." In addition, Davis missed more than a month with a knee injury. The Lakers finished 33–49 and missed the playoffs.

The Lakers have claimed 17 NBA championships. That ties them with the Celtics. They have also reached the Finals 15 other times. That's a total of 32 appearances! The Celtics are second, with 22. No other team has more than 12. From George Mikan to Kobe Bryant, the Lakers have showcased some of the NBA's greatest superstars. Fans can't wait to see who will lead the team to its next championship.

Malik Monk

INDEX

James Worthy